RESPONSORIALS

Rich Follett and Constance Stadler

NeoPoiesis Press, LLC

NeoPoiesis Press
P.O. Box 38037
Houston, Texas 77238-8037

www.neopoiesispress.com

Copyright © 2009 by Rich Follett and Constance Stadler

All rights reserved. No part of this book may be used or reproduced in any manner whatsoever without express written permission from the publisher except in the case of brief quotations embodied in critical articles and reviews.

Responsorials by Rich Follett and Constance Stadler
ISBN10 0-981-99843-7 (paperback : alk. paper)
    1. Poetry. I. Follett, Rich and Stadler, Constance

Printed in the United States of America.

First Edition

Contents

Foreword v
Introduction vii

Responsorial: Wing Spans

Vow (c.s.) 2
Entreaty (r.f.) 4

Responsorial: Rush Hour

Commute (c.s.) 8
Metro, Sexual (r.f.) 10

Responsorial: Irreconcilable Similarities

Boxes (r.f.) 14
Compost (c.s.) 16

Responsorial: Tobacco Road Pietà

Thusday's Chil' (c.s.) 20
Woe (r.f.) 25

Responsorial: Y?

Witzie (c.s.) 32
Richard 101 (r.f.) 34

Responsorial: ℞

11A, Ward 5 (c.s.) 38
Necromancy (r.f.) 40

Responsorial: Chivalry, Once Removed

Squiring Susie (r.f.) 46
Shining Knight (c.s.).. 49

Responsorial: In the Gloaming

Chowder Days (c.s.).. 54
Viaticum (r.f.) 56

Foreword

Alterity attracts. Attracts, especially when the binary opposites are the masculine and the feminine. There is an intense interest in the intersubjectivity of male and female, especially when the relationship has a concern with that occurrence that is designated by a fuzzy and imprecise word, "love."

We wonder about this "sweet mystery of life, "whether or not it is a reality or an illusion. Is our "love" merely a myth, a meme, a crystallization (Stendhal), or an empirical actuality, a real, unique, singular, particularized, corporeal event [I use the word <u>corporeal</u> in the sense of Maurice Merleau-Ponty and Roland Barthes--not street talk].

Now, how this word "love", from being faked has amassed so much monetary profit for popular song writers perplexes. What constitutes this state of existence - if it does exist - what is it that can be miracle and a marvel, or disaster and destruction? What is this state of being that can cause one to die for his or her beloved, or kill his or her beloved.

Biologists (Christopher Dawson, Daniel Dennett) would provide the scientific and thus reductive information that the origin of this human cherished value is the greed of a gene in its exclusive telos to reproduce itself. James Joyce in *Dubliners* has a character make the observation on the masculine-feminine relationship that a man can never be a friend with a woman because he will always want to have sex with her. In *Here to Eternity,* James Jones has a character make a similar observation: after a convivial, congenial philosophic conversations, she says to the man, "What all this means is that you want me to take off my dress." I have found one of the best descriptions of love in Rainer Maria Rilke, "Love is the cherishing of each other's solitude."

This book of poems *Responsorials* is not only exciting for their poetic art, but also for diverse responses to this alterity of man and woman. The reader will be moved by the sentiments, surprised, enlightened, baffled.

The attentive and intensified reader will pause, meditate, and become transformed. He will repeat what Rilke said after seeing Apollo's Torso, "I must change my life," by learning how to love, or how to stoically endure the despair of not loving.

Duane Locke

Introduction

What is most beautiful in virile men is something feminine; what is most beautiful in feminine women is something masculine. - Susan Sontag, *Against Interpretation*

    The complex relationship between masculine and feminine, explored consistently throughout the history of poetry, offers fertile ground for collaborative creation. In discussion of the inherent possibilities we realized with astonishment that, in a milieu where authenticity is venerated as a hallmark of quality, the lion's share of published poems exploring this duality have been written from a singular rather than a dialogical perspective. The poems in this collection represent a resultant ongoing effort to break free from the bonds of such limitations; specifically, this is a collection of poetic dyads (responsorials) intended to reveal the myriad facets of the masculine/feminine adventure.

    The imagined scenarios offered here have been structured to expose both the strengths and weaknesses of male/female relationships through a full diapason of emotion. To allow for maximum creative ebb and flow, each construct was initiated by one of us; the other worked without prior knowledge to craft a response based on first impressions of the work as received. As a result, we have been challenged to role play and to relax artistic boundaries, sacrificing creative authority. Authorship of respective works is indicated by a set of initials following each poem title. Whether the relationship is between a dysfunctional backwoods mother and her 'bad seed' son, a curmudgeonly hospice patient and his ebullient nurse, two commuters in the crush of both traffic and passing attraction or any other of a number of poetic personae, the emphasis has been on genuine interaction and discovery.

    In closing, we hope that these poems will entertain, provoke and move the reader. In addition, it is our sincere hope that our reflected journey will catalyze other writers to continue the collaborative process initiated here. We have been richly rewarded in our labors. This collection is lovingly dedicated to the anima and animus in each of us.

C.S. and R.F.

Responsorial:

Wing Spans

Vow (c.s.)

I give you my eyes.
No longer will
the remnant horrors
blind you
to the promised
vistas of verdant
dreams.

I give you these firm hands
that
have held the clapper
of the tolling bell.

I give you this back
that bears the stripes
of
conditioned abominations
retching destitution
despised, aborted, alone.
Rest upon me, my love.

I give you the luminous
and the transcendent
all that sanctifies this 'One'.
Yes, soul and soul
seamed together
in emboldened
purpled
tapestry
proclaiming
timeless
surety.

I give you my lips
warm,
sweet, aching passion
airbrushed baby's breath,
fingertips of lace
heralding the gift of the heart
so cherished.

Entreaty (r.f.)

Beloved,
my world
was endless emptiness and
            infinite isolation
until your light
warmed into oneness my nothingness
and from benighted desert
conjured an inexplicable, abundant harvest.

I, witness to and recipient of
            this measureless miracle,
can utter only grateful gibberish;

I
who dreamed of water
        when my mouth was full of sand
must watch bewildered as my blistered lips reanimate
and spill an arduous, aqueous 'amen'
to wash the feet of their redeemer.

You
have raised a dead man –
        have called back my extinguished heart –
and I, newborn in your tender affections,
have only bootless cries of ecstasy
            to tender for
                    immortality in your embrace.

Beloved,
is it any wonder I stand here amazed?

Through your grace
        I walk in sunlight;
through your caress
        my rough wounds are made smooth;

though your strength
    my squandered yesterdays become promised tomorrows;
through your blessed love
      I am,
          this day,
              before God,
finally
      and fully *alive*.

On this day
      of sacred, spirit-filled vows,
a question …

(it is time to take flight
      and my newfound feet are clay)

Summoning metamorphosis;
    severing umbilical solipsism
            I call inward –
                into the void of once-self

and Lazarus answers:

I do.

Responsorial:

Rush Hour

Commute (c.s.)

subway sway
so inviting
for a quick quiet drift
before the work week

        d
        e
        s
        c
        e
        n
        t

    the inner chatter
begins

'email check or coffee prep?'
'will he be pissy today?'
'Chinese for lunch?'

Feeling a purse-level graze
I instinctively snap to attention.
… a fumbled apology,
    cheeks reluctantly reddening
you seemed so out of place, of time …
I said, "It's alright, really"
    startled at my sincerity.

Meeting my gaze,
    you wish me a good day
I sense your desire to linger.
I feel pleasure in the knowing.

But steel doors slam apart and
    gobs of humanity swap.

For three more stops
                I wonder …

Metro, Sexual (r.f.)

What were the chances?

A lifetime of meaningless faces,
        a miasma of myriad anonymous encounters

and here,
        now,
            this morning,
                improbably, impossibly:

YOU.

I fancied myself
past the blush of happenstance attraction,

yet I flush with…

what?

Embarrassment?

Excitement?

Ecstasy?

Mouth snapped open as doors snapped shut, I

s
  p
   i
  r
 a
  l

into absurd social paralysis.

If only
        I could call out
                your name ...

Responsorial:
Irreconcilable Similarities

Boxes (r.f.)

Hands clasped, fingers casually entwined;
    the mediator is perplexed.
"Are you *sure* you want to go through with this?
        You two obviously still love each other …"

Her world is so simple,
    her perspective so pragmatic.

How many times she must
have   lif-
ted   the
veil   for
teary   eyed
coup   les
just   like
us   with
that efficient, doe-eyed query

as if we could pack up our answers for the move ahead …

One box (large) for depression;
    another (larger) for expectations;
        a third (very small) left empty for the love we felt sure
            would come
                (how much room does a spark need, anyway?) …

How many boxes might it take to hold
                seven years' worth of good intentions
                      and faulty reasoning?

"Yes," we say:
    (in unison, inexplicably synchronized –
        this has always been our chief impediment)
"we are sure."

What the mediator cannot know – could never comprehend –
   is how many boxes we had to *un*pack
      to sit here, across the table from her with
         hands clasped, fingers casually intertwined …

Compost (c.s.)

    So simple,
        so simple.
           We met, courted, wed.

Startled ourselves
    by the 'happy' of it
and possible
        content.

By the time we realized
something *had* to be done
        we knew

nothing possibly could.

    Numbness, vaporized 'family'
           'home'
undefined, disconnected, spectral
      hoverings o'er
    newly needed
        'private time'.

And when the chirpy counselor
assaulted with her grocery lists
    of marriage save 'to dos'

We laughed at her
    stunning incomprehension
      of what was

        so
            irrevocably
                true.

Wherever you are this day,
 I wish I knew
    what I would wish
  for you.

Responsorial:
Tobacco Road Pietà

Thusday's Chil' (c.s.)

Demons spew'd dat Wensday black
Dat night
       Dat
              curs'd night

curs'd laffin' wif th' dammed

Banshees rippin' sky threadbare
Furies spreadin' seed despair
Layin' bare they suckling feast

      mah faintes' ginger'd joys
      mah peach-canned hopes
        I took on God A'mighty
          in unholy offrins'
            desprit
                fo' th' savin'.

Th' sky whip catgut wet
Th' torrent, Hades' sweat
Rain coursin' deep, dat fever sweet
"Mah Love, mah Lam', may dese be th' only tears
        you evah know."
I press'd...
  ... a million, thousin' times
      threshin' in dat hemorrhaged troth;
            clampin' crucifix t' breast.

The doctor slapped
   "Bear down, bear down!!"
But no,
    "not yet!"
        I writh'd
You *mus'* be a Thusday chil'
No woe, no woe, no woe

Th' fiercest words dat evah wuz prayed
Dear Lawd, dis *mus'* be
                so …

I wep' in mah bindin's
   fo' th' mercy'f it
   tradin' soul wif' any taker
         fo'
              a kine o' dream

Later, delivered, dat bastard
        fum Perdition slime
came swayin' in cheap moonshine blind
Two nights an' a bit

den Lucifer ovah yo' cradle peered
in dat wick'd, loveless way
I knew wha' he'uz plannin'
              jes' waitin' fo' th' day

Months passed and th' murderin' dust
                  resettled
Dat death clock start in …
 tic
     toc
tic
  toc

I *smell*
fresh demon plague

Wif every step mo' toward mah babe
              th' stinkin' rot
          I
        runnin' mo' n' mo'

and den I sees
      th' bastard, danglin' mah babe in 'Polyon's clasp
          ovah attic window ledge
              wavin' *mah* chile, like a smoka' can -
                like coven incense.

O Lawd, mah God, mah Lawd, mah God!

dat wail of slaughter'd innocence,
dat yowlin' rage
   brandin' white hot pain,
I pass th' mountain top o' incompahenshen wild -

Jumpin,' I caught (praise Jesus)
      and curl'd roun' you
so white light tight
      you featha-fell on china fine moss
    I brick-gashed mah head but
      Yo' cooin' rais'd life from deafth.
   … dem angel voices
     cryin' out: "Hol' breafth,
           hole breaf,
              hole bref …"

In time, I saw you had mah eyes
     vacuous an' vacan' like
         th' loss dat sealed mah life.

When 'It' came back in,
      swaddlin' stench an' perpetooity o' whiskey drench,

a-gin,

    a-gin,

        a-gin …

tearin' off mah skirt,
        slammin' dat table back as
                I rake dem stone sin eyes
an you jes'
     stood dere
     stood by yo' Mama
             no cryin' lef' to cry
'mbeddin' graceless deafth march
             inta mah failin' heart.

Mah babe, mah babe, mah wound t' grave -
Yo' truck squeal as you brake.

(I'd hol' you fer a thousin'million years …)

I traced yo' ravine tears.
Yo' name, mah breafthless murmurin'
"No.
     No,
      don' leave
            me
                  Ma ..."
        Dis time
  you soaked th' quilt,
         dis time
            yo' heart bled so
But such wuz past mah grasp.
Mah Thusday chil,'
soon all alone, nowhere
                  t' go …

Mah son, mah son -

Mah livin' flesh

Mah gift o' sun, mah bliss

Aborted brefthful wisp ...

... mah' Wensday drownin' kiss;

Dat thunnerstorm
           had won ...

Woe (r.f.)

th' firs' one, mama –
      she smell like peaches n' ginger
            she'uz so *fine*, mama.

you'd a lik'd her jus' fine, too.

i know you woulda.

i close my eyes, i see'd you'n her t'gether in th'kitchin
   cannin' yo' jars n' clappin' like twin spikes a'heat lightnin'
             all steamy in th' sweet, syrupy air

an' when i hel' her, mama –
     she'uz makin' sof' noises in her neck – such *sof'* noises -
        an' she'uz a-squirmin' an' a-shimmyin' in th'dark
           like she 'uz made to be jus' wid me
                wid *me*, mama –
                    jus' wid *me*.

i try t' hol' her, mama – i try all night lon' but all i see'd
wuz you
you wuz tryin' t' hol' me back like you allus do
like you allus did

when i come inna th' worl', mama,
shithead say you nearly kill yo'sef on a Wenday
jus' tryin' t' hol' me back.

peaches n' ginger …

i tol' her all 'bout you, mama
i tol' her an' i hel' her an' i see'd th'light like a candle

i see'd *yo'* light comin' outta her eyes, mama
i watch'd it leave …

an' you wuzn' holdin' me back then, mama;
you wuz miles away, praise-prayin' n' murmurin' low:
"lawd Jesus, save my son –

no mo' woe, lawd, no mo' woe."

dat second girl, mama,
she wuz'n no account.

she try to hol' her legs together
like shithead allus say you done
before you'n him got me

she wuz'n no account
she wuz'n no trouble
she wuz'n much t' look at

but she smell like whuskey, mama
    jus' like you affer you been wid shithead
              so i couldn' let her stay

dat second one, mama -
    she wuzn' nothin'
        she wuz'n nuthin' like you.

an' dem others?
nobody know'd 'bout dem, mama.

only now, *yo'* gonna know
        yo' gonna go
            yo' gonna see

an' now i got woe, woe, n' mo' woe.

i never mean' fo' you t'see, mama.

        never mean' fo' you t' know.
            dey wuz jus' s'posed t'be wid *me*, mama -
                      jus' wid *me*
but now
        dey gonna be wid *you*
            yo' gonna leave me now
                'an yo' gonna see
                      what you wuz'n never s'posed t'see.

an' yo' gonna *know*, mama -
an' yo' gonna look down an' murmur
"lawd, save my son"

"no mo' woe, lawd, *no mo' woe*."

ain't nothin' i can do, mama
                ain't got no tears
                      i wuz born to woe
                              an' you allus tryin' t' hol' me back.

shithead knew, mama -
        knew 'bout th'storm
            knew 'bout th'doctor
                knew 'bout you squeezin' yo' legs t'gether

kindes' thing he ever done wuz try t'drop me
                          t'hol' me back
                                  an' *you* wouldn' let him

now, ain't *dat* sumpin'?

so i grew on accoun' a'you

an' now all dem girls
dey gonna get t'meet you at las' -

ride dat storm, mama,
ride dat storm;

dey all dere
    waitin' t' tell you, mama -
        tell you y' done rais'd up th'devil's own

an ever' one of 'em i done
    i done on a Wenday, mama, but
        i allus waited 'til Thursday t'give 'em back to th'earth
            ('cuz Thursday – da's *my* day)

nobody know'd

nobody even know *now*

but yo' gonna know, mama
    yo' gonna know
        real soon...

yo' gonna cry th' thunder
    yo' gonna scream th' lightnin'
        yo' gonna be a mighty storm, mama
            yo' gonna bring down th' rain
                yo' gonna try t'hol' me back

but you cain' say woe t' me no mo', mama –

no mo' woe.

Responsorial:

Y?

Witzie (c.s.)

You made the wheels turn
    on my Trailways bus
At the blue table
I snuck behind you
tickled your hand hey high
    (hush of a hush) "Eleven!"
After pretzels and milk
 we scrumbled together
    O!
  Happy Nap
And every buckle
    of my
yellow splosh galoshes
was duly fastened and puddle proof.

Oh, how
 we slid in those gutter
      slick
       oyster shells
of afterschool dirt drop dew …

… two score and some
 I take my car
    for the tiniest tweak,
you know, I'm gonna call.
And whenever the missus
      tosses that
        boondraggled keister
you'll be refuged and tucked
under cat-rippled ancient crochet.

We've hugged and wept at every birth.

  Held tight
  through
        all the gradient goodbyes.
And I still call you 'Witzie'
        when your wingtips
        illume an excess
           of success

Strange, I always answered "an only child"
Always knowing I was wrong.

Richard 101 (r.f.)

Just now, plucked from the routine I revere,
to hear again that name you made for me;
the silver'd chime of 'Witzie' in my ear
awakens cherished camaraderie.
I am no poet, nor am I at ease
with airy words your art would understand;
bereft of wings, I covet such release
as verses bring to those who weave their strand.
Amid lost crumbs of cookies, pride and dreams
I offer up a tear in recompense -
galoshes, oyster shells and dew, it seems
are echoes from when make-believe made sense.
Respectability can suffocate:
O, twin! That Trailways bus still warms the gate …

Responsorial:

11A, Ward 5 (c.s.)

Amidst tendrils of tubing
and massive megatronics
taking precise metric measure
of the last days of the life
              of
    hairless, fetal
    enfleshed bones.

I have come to wash you
Pat cream on bedsore
              infestations
and whisper
       that I am here.

We have been friends for almost
          three months.
Back then, I brought you broth
      and thinner cranberry juice
adjusting your bed height,
       plumping pillows 'til smile ...

And on those gifted nights
       played a hand or two of gin
turning Aerosmith up just
       an illegal notch or so ...

Witnessing the emptiness
As streams of loved ones
      walked blithely by ...
I slipped into your room
   to tuck a sheet,
     stroke your brow
       as you twisted in
         fitful
           sorrows.

I have seen this so many times
     I was sure that this had passed.
Yes,
 I dutifully check my level
              of steadfast.

… but oh,
      how I will miss …

Necromancy (r.f.)

Once, I was alive;

now, I am dying.

Bookends; yin and yang;

alpha and bitter omega

that no measure of poking, prodding

or peremptory platitude

can reconcile.

The glass *is* half empty,

you imbecile!

I no longer resemble

my former self;

you are a lousy liar.

I look like shit every day,

yet

you delight in telling me

I look well.

Do you really think

whispered aphorisms and

genial gestures

can buy me time?

I hate you

and your sterile,

medicinal magnanimity.

You are, quite simply,

the most cloying and calamitous woman

I have ever had the misfortune to know.

I am dying;

we both know I cannot live.

Why, then

(in infrequent intervals

of medically induced somnolence)

do I drift, dreaming

toward the white light

of your thighs?

Responsorial:

Chivalry, Once Removed

Squiring Susie (r.f.)

Beach blanket, fun-in-sun lakeside halcyon hours
               cascade even now in memory's clarion canon;
                      your carillon laughter was my joy.

Our parents doubly blessed in friendship;
mine, Bride and Groom;
yours, Best Man and Maid of Honor:
an animate photo album –
Paradise in a sun-kissed suburban subdivision.

Even at three
I, paragon of jejune chivalry,
heedless of your vantic vacuity,
lived only for the favor of your sweet smile;
thrilled solely to the trill of your expressed pleasure –
a nascent knight
in unseeing life-and-death agon with burgeoning truth
(your glee my token;
your coo, my crest).

Ignoring limp arms and listless leanings,
in callow ecstasy,
I played the parts of both patty and cake;
content in proximity;
lost in the blissful penumbra of adoration's sinister
simplicity.

Beneath the standard Hope
I vainly rode,
thinking only of your hand …

Later,
(why could it not have been later still?)
the emptiness behind the eyes would signify;
your inexorable, detestable decline would effloresce

and I, distraught and disconsolate,
would begin my unfathomable solitary trek to acceptance.

You, dear Susie,
      my Dulcinea –
           would never walk,
                never speak,
                    never *be*
                       like me.

Realization was a withering wind,
puncturing a summer Sunday –
the hiss of bee-stung balloons,
the death knell of innocence
and ecstasy's demise.

My mother, funereal, explained;
my world imploded.

Profound.
    Mental.
        Retardation.

What of joy?
What of our imagined tomorrows?

From that day onward,
my every step bespoke execution;
at five, the child condemned
was a weary, wasting shell.

Fast-forward to fourteen:
our parents' friendship guilt-blighted and bleeding;
one Easter morning,
a brief obligatory call
and a pained visit punctuated by unspoken remorse.
In the putrid air of repudiated resurrection,

I, your broken knight errant, fueled by helpless futility,
summoned vestigial valor
to reach across time for your hand ...

It was then
that the long-relinquished miracle – Susie's smile –
burned away, by degrees, my figurative death,

burnishing the wounded sword of my bitterness to
scintillating Excalibur;
it was then,
in that moment,
bathed in the sanctity of profoundest beaming grace –

my infant-martyred soul
at last
acquired spirit armor.

Shining Knight (c.s.)

If you stare at wallpaper long enough
Hyacinths will bloom
In the distilled quiet of no voice
The robin sings to you
and the absence of a stance,
                a step
frees cheeks and fingertips
to dance.

How much you taught me ...
... patty-cake is more than fun
when two hands clap for four ...
... a twirling beach ball makes a silver lake
                a wondrous carnival ...
and shorecastles *can* reach the sky
when the whitest of knights
fulfills his Lady's
                most demure delight!

You showed me 'more' not 'less'
You proved I *'had'* not *'lost'*
You shushed self-pitying whys
You made me laugh so much

that I

        forgot to cry.

When the boys sailed by
                with wild whirl kites
pointing at my chair
and girls made ugly faces
    the mimicry of *she,* piercing air with sound,
               agonistes unbound ...

You made them ashamed, disgraced
    by saying
how pretty my hair was
    as it blew across my face.

Oh my dearest friend, my Quixote –
how many windmills did you conquer
to make my loll, roll days
sun-kissed?

In time
the candle grew softer;
                I
swayed to the soft dimming light
  head hurting more and more
  release became my fight, my flight.

But having so much
from mommy, daddy
    and you
    I gently closed my eyes
in cotton-candy bliss
      awash in love and tenderness
... of 'missing' and of 'missed.'

We know you are a poet, so

    I tell you this rhyme true.

I see you
    as you teach your charges
      with wisdom, deep and hued.

I see you
    hold your loving wife
    with adoration blind

I've watched you seize the vilest evil
        and render it benign.

I behold you pen this ode to us;

      again,
two smiles

              entwine ...

Responsorial:

In the Gloaming

Chowder Days (c.s.)

A sunless dawn;
      the pregnant fog –
   white caps
     announce
          grey tide.

A day for chowder …
real cream and
butter,
brimming with
sweet meat.

A day as this has always
          comforted.
For in the years you
fought
the Axis and insanity
watching brothers blown
         to pieces
and you so blatantly alive,
I felt the world was aching
       as much as you –
       as much as I.

I can see your silhouette
with fishing pole
totally unaware of bend
         or sway
or any sign of
      sportsman's play;
you're back with Mackie
         and
          Little Mike
and Sarge right as he fell.

You will come back to me
   as you have
      for better than
         half a century.

And I will
      light soft hurricane lamps;
 feed you the richest chowder;
         rub away all the chill …

… and you will look at me
            through stars.

Viaticum (r.f.)

Then,
    as now, my beloved,
        (some sixty years on)

I let my thoughts drift to you
    in a white cotton nightgown …
billowing guilelessly in effortless gossamer grace;
    illuminating even the most mundane morning rituals …

parting the curtains,
    peeling potatoes,
        preparing chowder –

you were,
    you *are*
        the only poetry my life has known or needed.

When the war raged;
    when the bombs fell;
        as my banded brothers
            found Heaven's gate;
                day after hellish day –
every wisp of cloud-white gunsmoke,
        every white-hot spray of shrapnel
was a fold in your white cotton gown –
    a sail come to waft me away
        to the sweetness of our chowder days
            and
remembered home.

Lately,
I am in need of your billowing sails more and more;

I meander aimlessly through rivers of memory –
        through fields of echoed agony undimmed by time –
scanning the howling horizon for any sign of peace,
hungering for release.

Soon, I think, it will be time
        for billowed sails and safe harbor;

until then,
        light your lamp, my white-winged angel –
        stir once more your sacred stovetop salvation:

I will fight for one more day;
I will shout back the darkness;
I will crawl on my belly through the killing fields;

all for the touch of your hand …
all for the poetry of your white cotton gown …
all for the chance to savor your chowder –

rich;
creamy;
sweet;

life itself –
        and you

the giver.

Constance Stadler has been writing, publishing, and editing poetry from the 'prehistoric' epoch of print journals to modern e-times. She was a former editor of *South and West* and is currently a contributing editor to the e-zine *Eviscerator Heaven* and Review Editor for *Calliope Nerve*. She has published over 300 poems and three chapbooks in her 'first manifestation' as a poet, and has just released her first two chaps in 20 years, *Tinted Steam* (Shadow Archer Press) *Sublunary Curse* (Erbacce) and an eBook, *Paper Cuts* (Calliope Nerve Media).

Her most recent work appears in such 'zines as *BlazeVox, ditch, ken*again, Pen Himalaya, Rain Over Bouville, Clockwise Cat, Unlikely Stories 2.0, Hanging Moss, Neonbeam,* and *Gloom Cupboard*. Recently, she has been 'Featured Poet' for the *Guild of Outsider Writers, Counterexample Poetics* and *The Poetry Warrior*.

Rich Follett is an actor, musician and teacher who has recently returned to writing poetry after a thirty-year hiatus. A founding member of the Shenandoah Valley's premiere poetry group The Aubade Circle, his work has been published in several issues of *Paraphilia* and *Calliope Nerve* and in a 'Featured Poet' capacity at *Counterexample Poetics*. Rich has been repeatedly recognized for his artistry in spoken word, most notably at the inaugural summer poetry festival in Middletown, Virginia and on blog talk radio. The poet Duane Locke has publically recognized the excellence of his poetic artistry.

Duane Locke holds a Ph.D in English Renaissance Literature and was Professor of English and Poet in Residence at the University of Tampa for over twenty years. Locke, has, who has published 6,379 different poems in print magazines, e-zines, and books, has two books published this year 2009, *Yang Chu's Poems* by the Canadian publisher Crossing Chaos, and *Voices from a Grave* by British publisher, Erbacce.

Steve Viner lives in Dorset, UK, with his wife, Donna, and daughter, Athene. He has illustrated several chap books for Shadow Archer Press, including *Tinted Steam* for Constance Stadler, with another cover to be released in the near future.
Steve has had work shown in *The Glasgow Review* as well as various other e-zines and has held a successful Exhibition in the UK.

A free audio recording of this book
is available for download at
http://www.neopoiesispress.com/23712.html

NeoPoiesis
a new way of making

in ancient Greece, poiesis referred to the process of making
creation – production – organization – formation – causation
a process that can be physical and spiritual
biological and intellectual
artistic and technological
material and teleological
efficient and formal
a means of modifying the environment
and a method of organizing the self
the making of art and music and poetry
the fashioning of memory and history and philosophy
the construction of perception and expression and reality

NeoPoiesis Press
reflecting the creative drive and spirit
of the new electronic media environment

www.ingramcontent.com/pod-product-compliance
Lightning Source LLC
Chambersburg PA
CBHW060503110426
42738CB00055B/2602